On the
BEACH

Joyce Hannam

Oxford University Press

Nobody in the hotel liked Spiros. He was the manager, but he was very unfriendly.

'I don't know why mum and dad wanted to come here,' thought Alex. 'They don't like holidays by the sea, they don't like this hotel, and they don't like Spiros. It's very strange.'

The hotel was on a small island in Greece. There were only a few other guests. There was an Italian, Vincenzo, who nobody saw much. He had a boat and he went sailing most of the time.

There were two Spanish girls, Luisa and Trini. Then there was Jean, a Frenchman, who spent all the time taking photos of his wife, Véronique.

'How stupid!' thought Alex. 'They must be just married.'

2

● Here are all the guests in the hotel. Which one is Vincenzo? Can you find Luisa and Trini? And Jean and Véronique?

3

Alex was American, but his parents, Panos and Eleni, were Greek. When Alex was very young, they moved from Greece to New York and opened an art gallery. Usually they stayed in big, expensive hotels in places like Rome or Paris. 'So why are we staying on this little island,' thought Alex, 'with an unfriendly man like Spiros?'

One morning Alex woke up early. All the other guests were asleep and the hotel was silent.

'I'll go for a walk along the beach,' he thought. 'Perhaps I'll see some new birds at this time of the morning.' Alex was very interested in birds, so he took his binoculars and started to walk along the beach.

It wasn't too hot at that time of the morning, and the sun was shining softly. Alex started watching the birds with his binoculars. Suddenly he saw a big group of birds together, close to the sea. There was something lying near the water. It looked like ...

'A body!' said Alex out loud. He suddenly felt cold and lonely in the sunshine. 'I must go and look,' he thought.

When he was close to the body, Alex stopped. He was afraid to look at the man. There was some blood on the sand.

'He met someone here,' thought Alex. 'Someone who came by boat.'

- How does Alex know this?

'The person came by boat because the footprints in the sand come from the sea,' thought Alex.

At last he looked at the man's face. It was white, and the eyes were open, but empty. Alex knew who the dead man was.

'Spiros!'

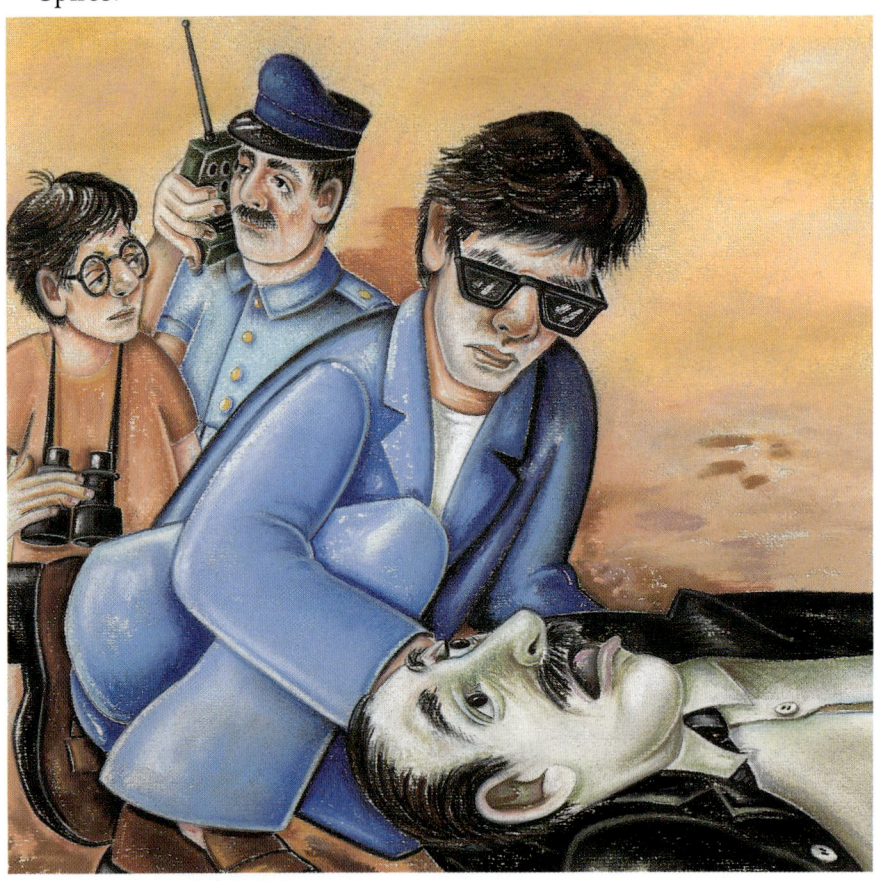

The police didn't need to look at the body for long.

'It was murder,' said the police chief. 'He was shot.'

When they came back to the hotel, the guests were all in the dining room. They knew that something was wrong.

'Spiros Andropoulos is dead. He was murdered,' said the police chief. 'Nobody can leave the island until we find the killer.'

There was silence. The policemen left.

As soon as the door closed behind the last policeman, everyone started shouting at once. It was hard to hear what anyone said.

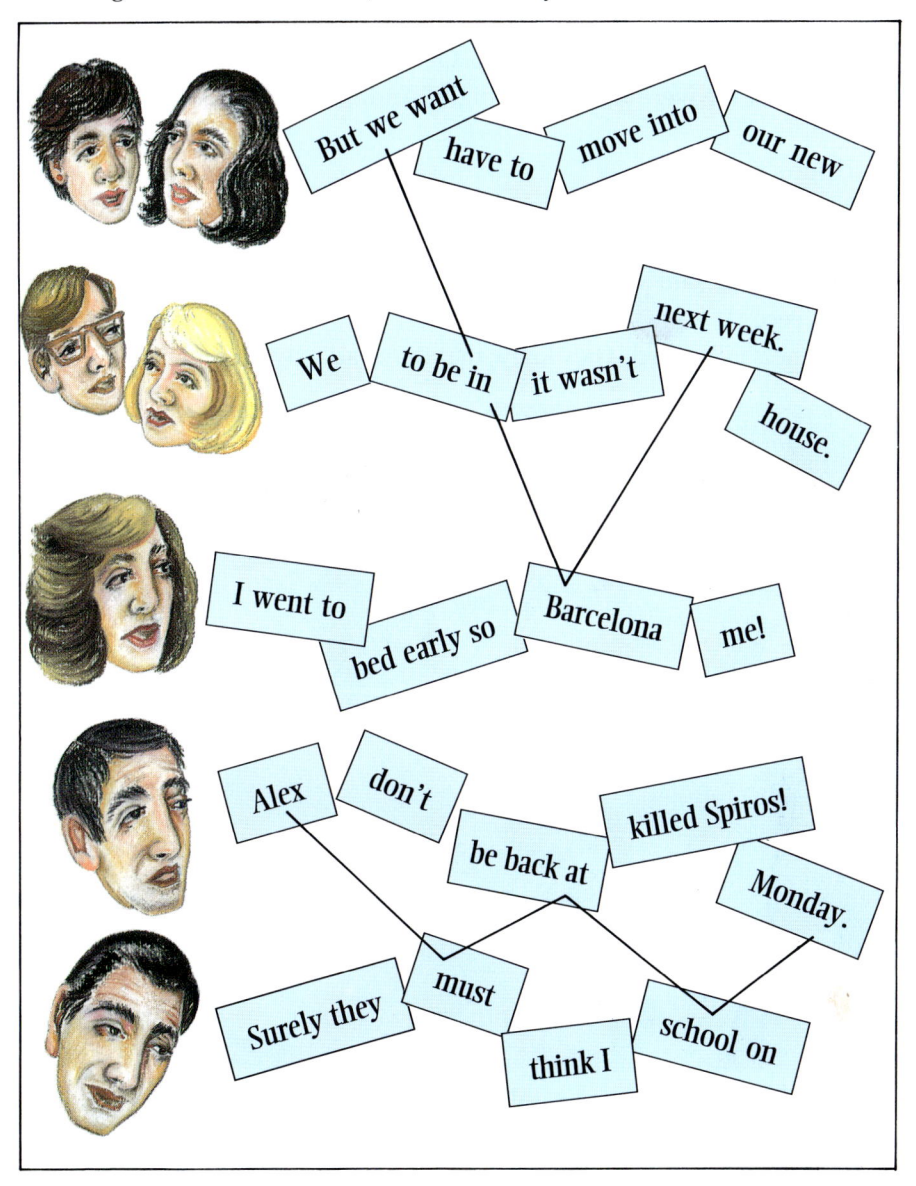

But we want to move into our new house.

We have to be in it wasn't next week.

I went to Barcelona me!

bed early so

Alex don't killed Spiros!

be back at Monday.

Surely they must school on

think I

● Can you understand what each person said?

7

'Stop shouting everyone!' said Alex. 'We must help the police to find the killer!'

The room was silent.

'The police are only doing their job. Of course they think that one of us killed Spiros. We were all here last night. And nobody liked Spiros, did they?'

No one said a word.

'But *somebody* killed him. We must try to find that person, to show the police that we have done nothing wrong. Do you agree?'

'Alex is right,' said Vincenzo. 'If we don't find the real killer, we can't leave Greece.'

The others all agreed. They knew that they had to work together.

'What shall we do first, Alex?' asked Luisa.

'We must try to answer the four big questions in any murder: *When? How? Who?* and *Where?* First, *when* was Spiros killed? Can anyone help?'

They all thought hard. Suddenly Luisa stood up. She was very excited.

'Trini,' she said, 'don't you remember the noise we heard last night? When we were on the balcony.'

'Yes, of course,' said Trini. 'How terrible! I never thought . . .'

'What?' asked Véronique. 'Tell us quickly. What did you hear?'

● They thought that they heard all these noises. Which one was really a gun?

'We heard a bang. We thought it was the noise of a motor bike.'
'What time did you hear this?' asked Alex.
'Well,' answered Trini, 'we left the disco when it closed ... about one o'clock. We walked slowly back to the hotel with two Greek friends. Then Luisa and I sat and talked on the balcony for some time before we heard the noise. So I think it was about two o'clock.'
'So Spiros was shot around two in the morning,' said Alex.
'But who shot him?' asked Véronique. 'It was dark, so the killer was close to Spiros.'

'The killer came from a boat. I saw his footprints in the sand. We must find that boat.'

'I think I can help,' said Vincenzo. 'There was a new yacht here last night. But this morning it was gone. I know all about boats, so I think I can remember what it was like.'

- The first picture shows the sea the evening before Spiros was murdered. The second picture shows the sea the next morning. One of the yachts went away during the night. Which one?

Vincenzo thought hard. 'It was . . . a red yacht with a blue and white flag. Yes, I'm sure! And there was a man on the yacht. He had long red hair. I know most of the people who sail round here, but he was a stranger.'

Alex was very excited. 'So we are looking for a man with long red hair, who has a red yacht with a blue and white flag. We are doing very well!'

'Are we?' said Jean. 'Who was the man on the boat and why did he want to kill Spiros?'

Nobody spoke. There was no answer to Jean's question.

Then Panos, Alex's father, looked at his wife.

'We must tell them, Eleni,' he said.

'You're right.'

'You see, we didn't come here for a holiday. We came to see Spiros.'

'I knew it!' said Alex. 'Is it because of the art gallery?'

'Yes,' answered his father. 'A few months ago we bought a painting. We thought it was an unknown painting by Picasso, found in Greece. It was Spiros who brought the painting to our gallery.'

'We have always wanted a Picasso,' said Eleni. 'So we paid a lot of money for it.'

'But a few weeks later we went to a gallery in Paris where there were lots of Picassos. Then we knew that our painting wasn't a *real* Picasso. It was just a good copy.'

- Look at the paintings in the Paris gallery. The picture on page 12 is a copy of one of these paintings. Which one?

'We knew that Spiros had a flat in Athens,' explained Eleni, 'because his address was on his suitcase when he came to the gallery. We wrote to him, but he never answered. So we decided to go there.'

'No one in Athens knew where he was. We spoke to a woman who lived in the same building.'

> Mr Spiros left on Tuesday afternoon. He has gone back to his hotel. He has a hotel on one of the islands, but I don't know which one. He went by plane. He had to catch the plane on Tuesday, because there wasn't another one until Thursday.

'This was very useful,' explained Panos. 'We looked at the flight schedule to find the times of planes to the islands. That was how we knew which island Spiros's hotel was on.'

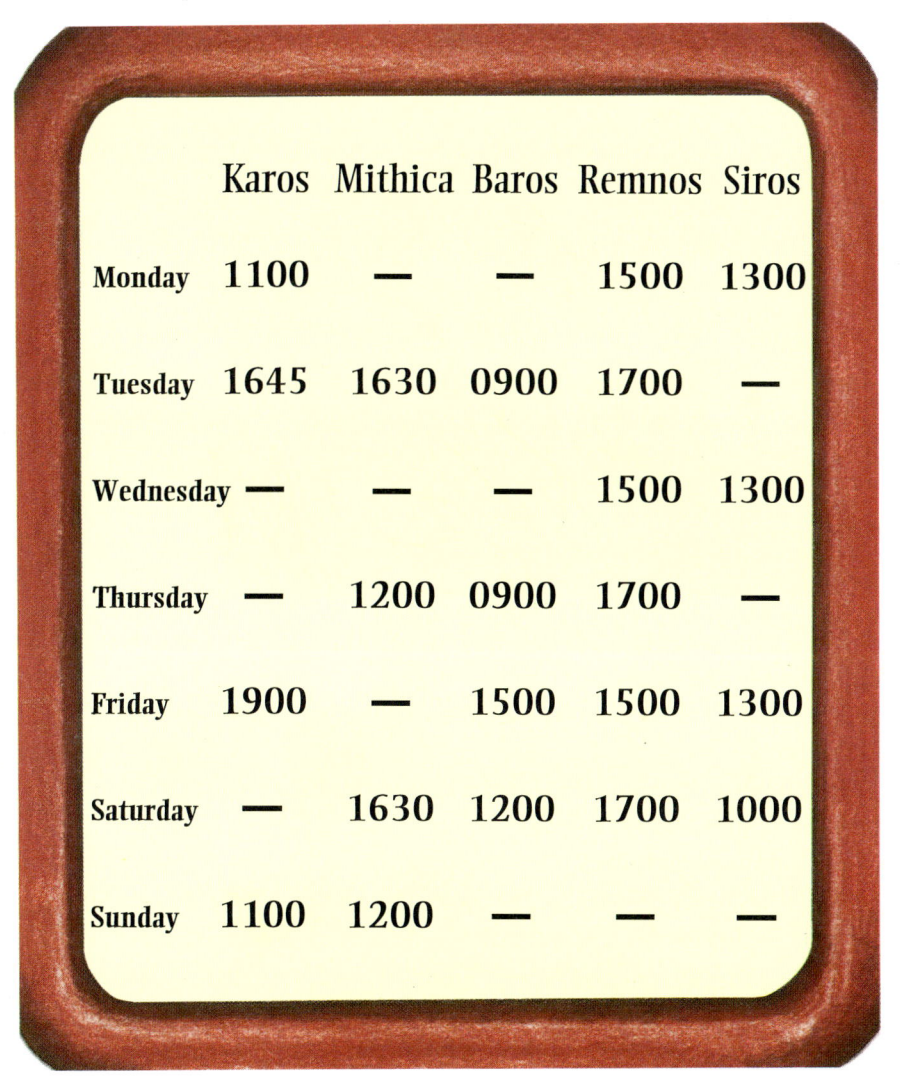

	Karos	Mithica	Baros	Remnos	Siros
Monday	1100	—	—	1500	1300
Tuesday	1645	1630	0900	1700	—
Wednesday	—	—	—	1500	1300
Thursday	—	1200	0900	1700	—
Friday	1900	—	1500	1500	1300
Saturday	—	1630	1200	1700	1000
Sunday	1100	1200	—	—	—

- Look carefully at what the woman says on page 14 and look at the flight schedule. Which island did Spiros go to?

'Once we arrived in Mithica it was easy to find Spiros, because this is the only hotel on the island.'

'What did he say when you told him that the painting was a copy?' asked Jean.

'He got angry. He said that it *was* a Picasso. But we knew this wasn't true. You can see that this hotel is full of copies of famous paintings.'

'Did Spiros paint them?'

'No,' said Panos, 'I think he just sold them for somebody. If we can find the painter, I think we will understand why Spiros was murdered.'

'Everyone must think hard,' said Alex. 'Has anyone seen a man painting near here?'

'Yes!' said Véronique. 'Don't you remember, Jean, when we went on that boat trip? We saw a painter on one of the islands.'

'When was this?' asked Vincenzo.

'Last week,' Jean answered. 'The trip goes to all the islands near here. There was a man painting on the third island.'

'Not the third,' said Véronique, 'the fourth.'

'Which islands did you visit?' asked Alex. 'Do you know their names?'

'No,' answered Jean.

'It doesn't matter,' said Vincenzo. 'I have a very good map of all the islands. I use it all the time. Just tell me something about the island.'

'It was a rocky island,' said Jean, 'and there was a beach. There were four or five houses and some fruit trees.'

'Orange trees, I think,' said Véronique. 'I didn't see any restaurants. Did you?'

'No. I think there was a very small church, but I'm not sure.'

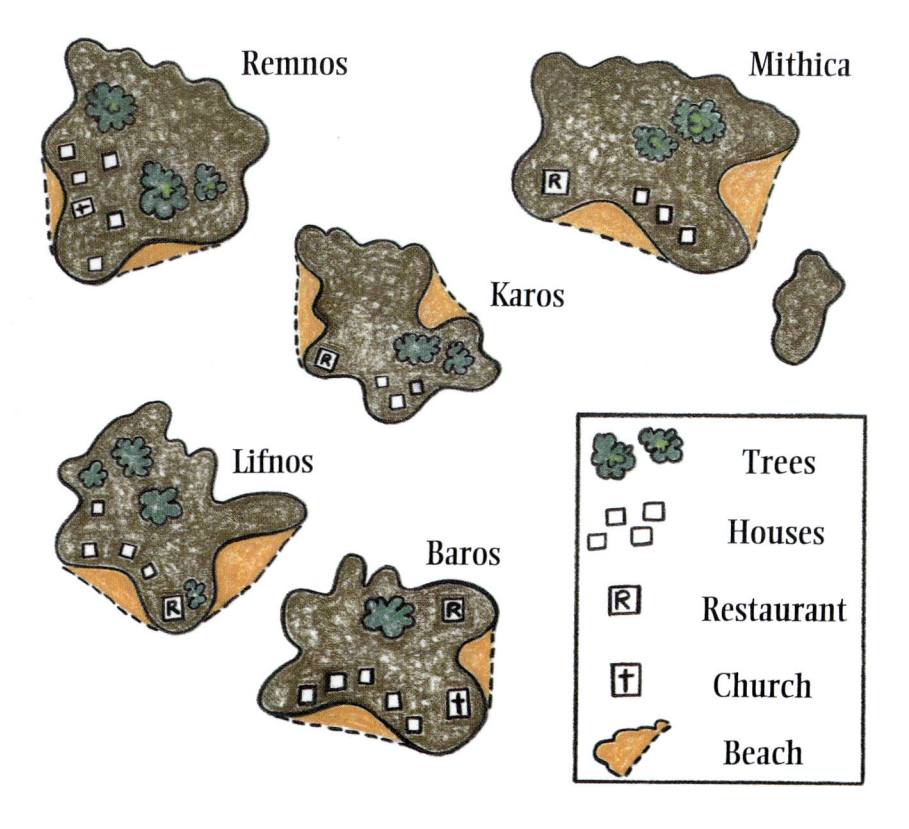

- Look at Vincenzo's map. On which island did Jean and Véronique see the painter?

'That's the island: Remnos!' said Vincenzo. 'Let's go there now. I've got a small boat. We'll take that.'

Alex turned to Trini and Luisa. 'Will you come with us? I've got a plan, but I'll need your help.'

Soon they were near Remnos.

'There are only a few houses on the island,' said Vincenzo. 'It will be easy to find the painter's house.'

'So what's your plan, Alex?' asked Luisa. 'When we find the painter, will you ask him if he knows Spiros?'

'No,' said Alex. 'That's too dangerous. Here's my plan: when we find his house, I want you to knock at the door and talk to him. Stay with him and make him talk for as long as possible.'

'I'll ask him about his work. I'll say that we saw him painting last week.'

'Very good!' said Alex. 'At the same time, I will go to the back of the house and get in somehow. I'll look for something which shows us that he knows Spiros – a letter or a note – something we can give the police to make them believe us. I'll probably need about ten minutes. Is that all right?'

'Don't worry,' said Luisa. 'Trini is very good at talking! The only problem will be to stop her after ten minutes. You will have lots of time to look around.'

'O.K. everybody,' said Vincenzo. 'But first we must find the house.'

They sailed past the island very slowly. Alex looked at the houses through his binoculars.

'There!' said Alex suddenly, pointing at one of the houses. 'That is the painter's house.'

'Which one?' asked Trini.

● Look at the houses in the picture. Alex knew immediately which was the painter's house. Do you know? Look again at the picture on page 2.

'How do you know?' asked Vincenzo.

'Don't you remember the painting in the hotel? It shows a garden with a little church, just like that one. The artist was sitting outside his house when he painted it.'

Vincenzo found a beach, not far from the painter's house.

'I'll wait for you all here,' he said. 'I'll be ready to leave as soon as you come back.'

The others got out of the boat and climbed the hill. They soon arrived at the road to the artist's house. Trini and Luisa went to the house, while Alex hid in some trees and watched. Trini knocked at the door and the painter came out – a man with long red hair!

Alex walked quietly round to the back of the house. The door was open.
'I'll try upstairs first,' he thought.

He went into the first room on the left. It was the painter's bedroom. There was nothing interesting there. Next to that there was another door. It was a bedroom too, but there was a second door inside the room.

Alex tried the door. It was locked. Where was the key?

- The key is hidden somewhere in the room. Can you find it?

Alex found the key under the clock. The door to the second room opened quickly and easily.

'This door is often used,' thought Alex.

A strong smell of paint came from inside the room. It was a large bright room with big windows. There were lots of paintings, lying against the walls. In the middle of the room was a painting that Alex knew. It was only half finished, but it looked like a Picasso. 'The police will want to see that,' he thought. 'I'll take it.'

He ran downstairs to look for other things to show the police. On a desk in the corner he found an old letter.

are here in the
asking a lot of
becoming too
me 2,000,000 drachmas

De

The Americans
hotel. They are
questions. It is
dangerous. Give

them everything.
Come late, because
to see us.

or I'll tell
Meet me tonight
I don't want them
Spiros

you
si

● Can you read the letter? What did Spiros want the painter to do?

'Now I understand,' thought Alex. 'The painter's name is Nick. Spiros wanted money from him.'

At that moment he heard voices from outside the house.

'You girls must come in and have a drink with me,' said a man's voice – Nick!

'That's very kind of you,' said Luisa, 'but we have to go now. Our friend is waiting for us in his boat.'

'I'm sure that your friend can wait a few minutes,' said the man. 'Please come in.'

Alex saw the front door begin to open. He ran to the back door. There was a big dog standing there. It barked angrily. He couldn't leave.

'Oh no! How am I going to get out?'

- How can Alex get out of the house?

He ran upstairs, through the bedroom and out of the window to the balcony. He jumped into the tree, then down onto the road behind the house.

'I must hurry,' he thought. 'When Nick goes back upstairs, he will see that his painting has gone. Then he will try to find me.'

At the same time, Luisa and Trini said goodbye to Nick.

'We must go now. Our friend is waiting. But thank you for talking to us.'

They began walking down the road to the beach.

'Do you think that Alex has already left?' asked Luisa.

'You heard the dog, didn't you? I'm sure that he left by the back garden.'

They were almost at the boat when they heard a shout behind them. It was Nick.

'He's coming after us, Trini. Quick!'

They ran to the boat. Alex was already there. Vincenzo started the engine and the boat sailed out to sea.

Nick was now on the beach.

'He's got a gun!' said Alex. 'Everyone down!'

A shot hit the back of the boat. But they went on out to sea, as fast as possible. They heard another shot.

'We are lucky,' said Vincenzo. 'That was very close.'

But a few minutes later the engine stopped.

'He hit the petrol tank!' said Vincenzo. 'And now it's empty. I haven't got any more petrol in the boat.'

'Oh no!' said Luisa. 'How will we get back?'

● They are still five kilometres from the hotel. The sun is starting to go down. How can they get back to the hotel before dark? Look carefully at the boat.

27

'I have some oars,' said Vincenzo. 'We will have to row the boat. Come on!'

Back at the hotel, the police chief was very angry.
'I told you all to stay on the island. I don't believe your story about a painter with red hair. If the others don't come back soon, you will be very sorry.'

Suddenly Eleni pointed out to sea.
'Look! There's a boat. It's moving very slowly, but it looks like Vincenzo's boat.'
'Send out the police boat,' said the police chief. 'Go and see who it is.'

Ten minutes later Alex and the others were back in the hotel. Alex showed the police chief the half-finished painting, and the letter from Spiros.

'I believe you now,' said the police chief. 'Spiros wanted to tell your parents about the paintings, so Nick killed him.'

He told two of his men to go to the island and find Nick. 'Thank you, everybody. You can go now.'

They all smiled.

'Let's spend our last night in Greece in the restaurant,' said Eleni. 'We'd like to buy you all a meal, to thank you for your help. Then we'll go back to New York – to our gallery of *real* paintings.'

Glossary

art gallery   a sort of museum where you can see paintings and sometimes buy them

balcony   a small platform on the outside of a house, in front of a window

bang   a loud, sharp noise, like the noise of a gun

bark (v)   to make a noise like a dog

copy (n)   a **copy** of a picture is another picture which is exactly the same

dining room   a room where people eat

engine   the machine in a car or boat which makes it move

excited   very happy; not calm or quiet

flag   all the boats on page 11 have a coloured **flag** on the top, flying in the wind

flight schedule   a list of aeroplanes with the times when they leave

footprint   when you walk on the beach, your feet leave **footprints** in the sand

guest   a person staying at a hotel

locked   shut with a key

manager   the most important person working in a hotel

motor bike   a sort of bicycle with an engine that makes it go fast

oars   long pieces of wood used to make a boat move

painter   a person who does paintings

painting   a picture made with different colours

parent   mother or father

petrol   a car or a boat will stop if there is no more **petrol** in the **petrol tank**

police chief   the most important policeman in a town

rocky   with lots of big stones or rocks

row (v) /rəʊ/   to make a boat move, using two oars

sand   very small pieces of rock on the beach; sand is usually yellow

shine   to produce light

sunshine   bright light from the sun

trip   a short journey

yacht   a boat with a sail which is pushed by the wind

Answers to the puzzles

page 3
(See illustration on page 31.)

page 7
Trini and Luisa: But we want to be in Barcelona next week.
Jean and Véronique: We have to move into our new house.

Eleni: I went to bed early so it wasn't me.
Panos: Alex must be back at school on Monday.
Vincenzo: Surely they don't think I killed Spiros!

page 9
The noise of the motor bike was really a gun.

page 13
Picture number 3

page 15
Mithica. There is a plane to Mithica on Tuesday afternoon and on Thursday, but not on Wednesday.

page 23
The Americans are here in the hotel. They are asking a lot of questions, It is becoming too dangerous. Give me 2,000,000 drachmas or I'll tell them everything. Meet me tonight. Come late, because I don't want them to see us. Spiros

page 3
1 – Véronique   2 – Jean   3 – Vincenzo   4/5 – Luisa and Trini

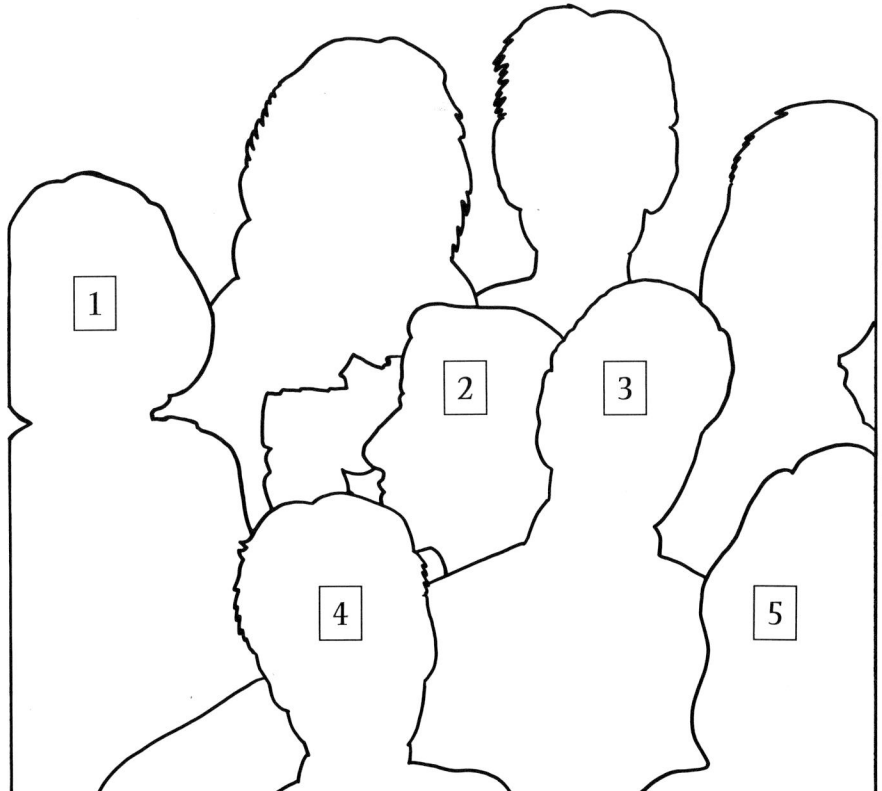

Oxford University Press, Walton Street, Oxford OX2 6DP

Oxford   New York
Athens   Auckland   Bangkok   Bogota   Bombay
Buenos Aires   Calcutta   Cape Town   Dar es Salaam
Delhi   Florence   Hong Kong   Istanbul   Karachi
Kuala Lumpur   Madras   Madrid   Melbourne
Mexico City   Nairobi   Paris   Singapore
Taipei   Tokyo   Toronto

and associated companies in
Berlin   Ibadan

OXFORD and OXFORD ENGLISH are trade marks
of Oxford University Press

ISBN 0 19 422486 4

© Oxford University Press 1994

First published 1994
Third impression 1996

No unauthorized photocopying

All rights reserved. No part of this publication may be reproduced, stored in a retrieval system, or transmitted, in any form or by any means, electronic, mechanical, photocopying, recording, or otherwise, without the prior written permission of Oxford University Press.

This book is sold subject to the condition that it shall not, by way of trade or otherwise, be lent, resold, hired out, or otherwise circulated without the publisher's prior consent in any form of binding or cover other than that in which it is published and without a similar condition including this condition being imposed on the subsequent purchaser.

Illustrated by Sue Sluglett

Printed in Hong Kong

For Christopher